Akbar called his ministers to a meeting – but he did not tell Birbal.

"Tomorrow," he said to them, "you must all come to me with an egg hidden in a pocket."

The ministers bowed low.

"Birbal, my chief minister, will come tomorrow as well," said Akbar. "Do not show him the eggs."

The ministers bowed low again.

King Akbar's Trick

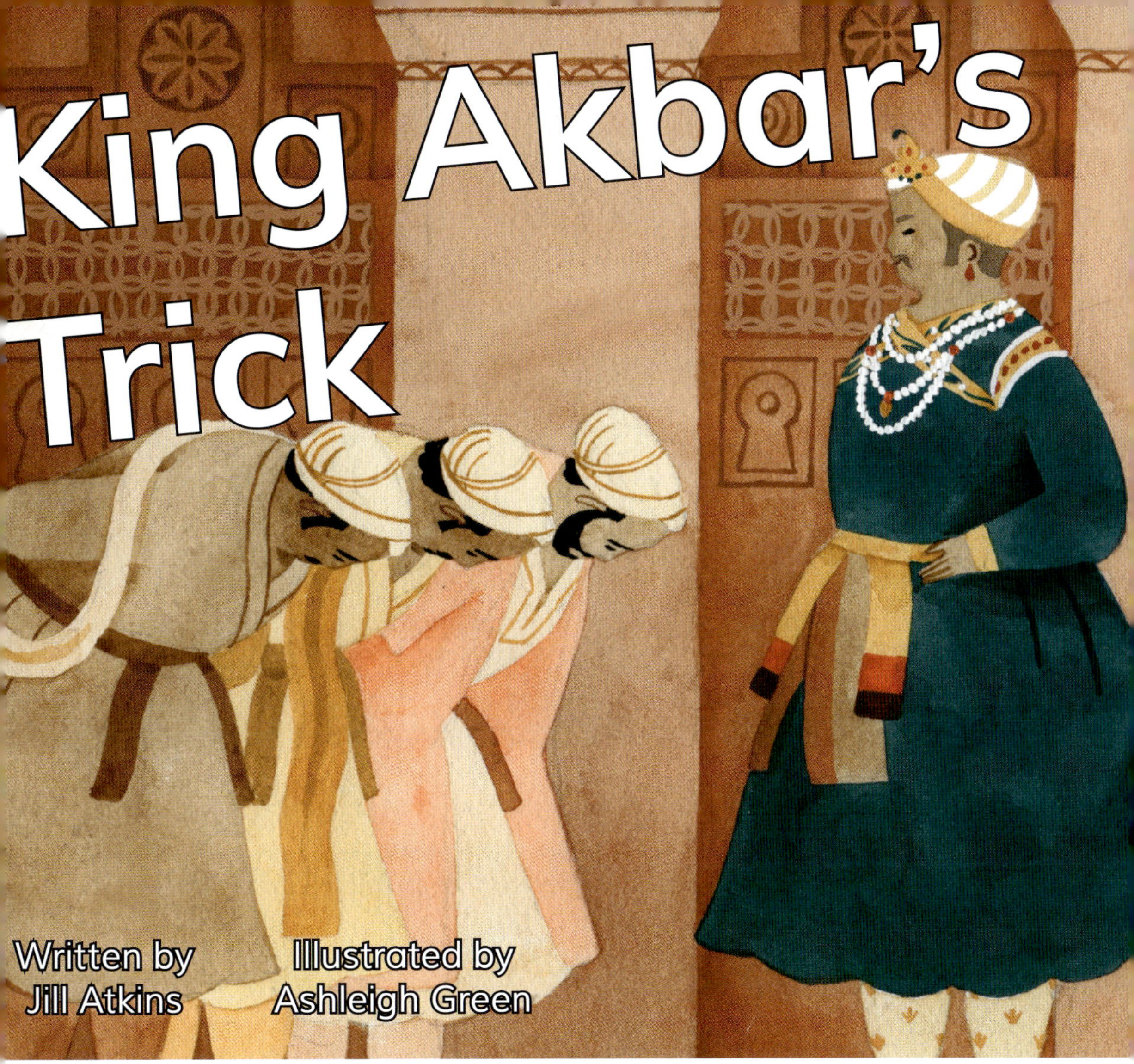

Written by
Jill Atkins

Illustrated by
Ashleigh Green

Published in 2026 by
Norwood House Press
2544 Clinton Street
Buffalo, NY 14224

Printed in the United States of America

Library of Congress Cataloging-in-Publication Data:
Names: Atkins, Jill (Children's author). | Rickard, Stephen, 1957-, author. | Green, Ashleigh, illustrator.
Title: King Akbar's trick / written by Jill Atkins, illustrated by Ashleigh Green. In the land of the midnight sun / by Stephen Rickard.
Description: Buffalo, NY : Norwood House Press, 2026. | Series: Phonics all-stars: phase 5b
Identifiers: ISBN 9781978578418 (pbk.) | ISBN 9781978578425 (library bound) | ISBN 9781978578432 (ebook)
Subjects: LCSH: Reading--Phonetic method--Juvenile literature. | English language--Phonetics--Juvenile literature. | Practical jokes--Juvenile fiction. | Polar regions--Juvenile literature.
Classification: LCC LB1573.3 A796 2026 | DDC 372.465--dc23

CPSIA compliance information: Batch #CW26NHP: For further information contact Norwood House Press at 1-800-237-9932.

Way back in time, there was a king named Akbar.

He was rich and had many important ministers.

His chief minister was called Birbal.

"I'm so fond of Birbal," Akbar said to himself, "but it might be fun to play a trick on him."

The next morning, Birbal and King Akbar's ministers came to the meeting.

"Last night, I had a dream," said the king. "You must each bring to me an egg from the king's pond. This will show me how much I can trust each of you."

The king stood at the window as the ministers all laughed and went down to the pond.

They all seemed to be hunting for eggs. One was in a rowing boat and one was hunting in the field next to the pond.

They seemed to be having a good time – apart from Birbal. He looked upset.

When they came back, each of the ministers held an egg.

Birbal, however, had no egg.

"Where did you get those eggs?" he asked.

"You didn't see them?" said one minister. "There were loads."

"Thank you all," called King Akbar. "You are good, true ministers. But, Birbal, I cannot see an egg ... "

All of a sudden, Birbal started crowing like a rooster. He crowed louder and louder.

The king looked confused.

"What is all this crowing for?" he asked.

Birbal laughed.

"I'm not a hen, my lord," he said, "so I do not have an egg for you. I am a rooster – and this is what I do best."

Then he started crowing again.

The king and all his ministers laughed.

"You are indeed my best minister, Birbal," said King Akbar. "You are such a clever one, too!"

"I played a mean trick on you, and I hoped to make you look foolish," King Akbar added. "But you showed me up with such quick thinking. Let that be a lesson to all of us!"

In the Land of the Midnight Sun

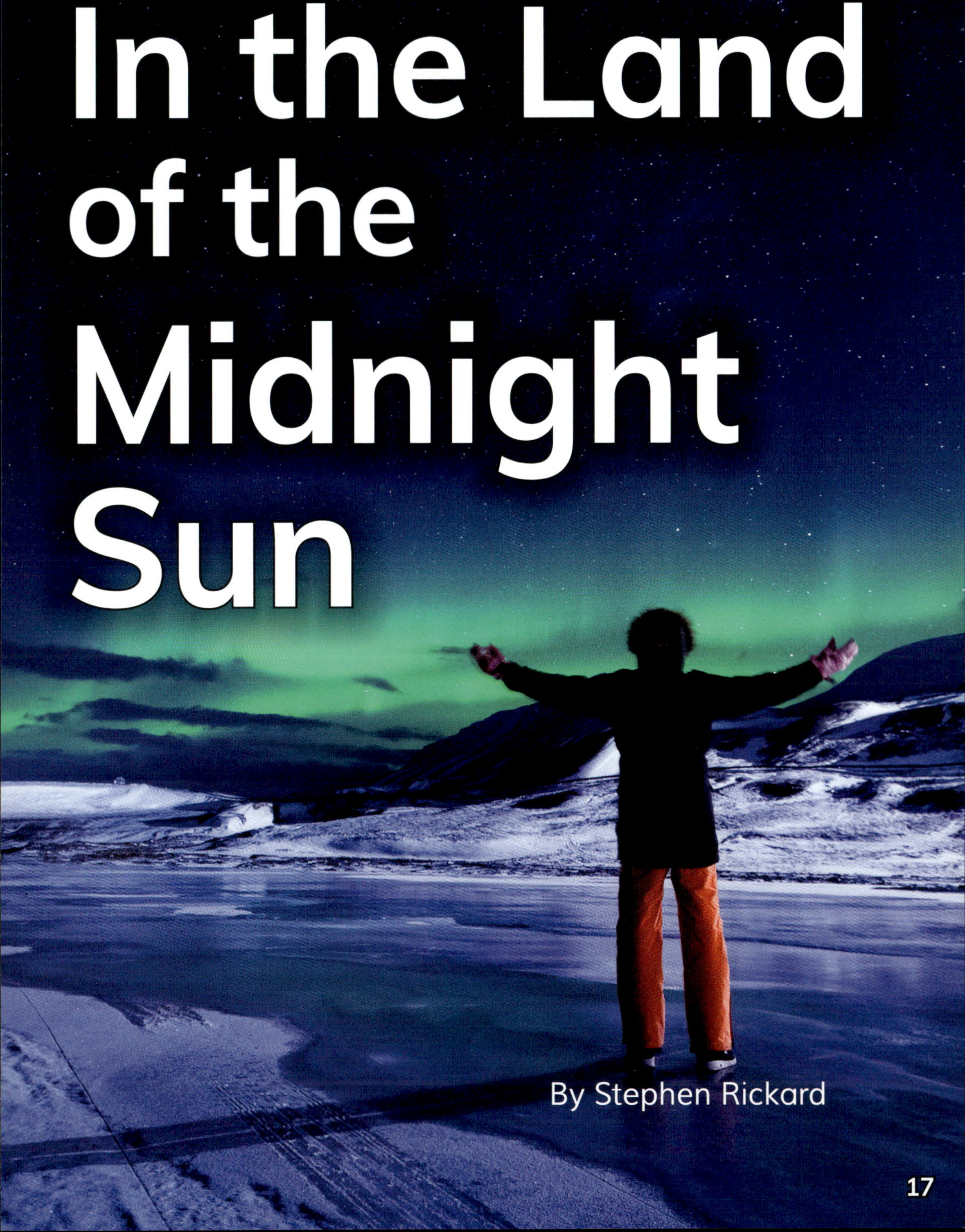

By Stephen Rickard

In the wintertime, our days are shorter than they are in the summertime.

It gets light later in the morning and, at the end of the day, it gets dark sooner.

It is colder too.

As you go further from the equator, the winter days get even shorter.

If you go as far as the Arctic or the Antarctic, then, in the wintertime, you may never see the sun.

This is because the sun might stay below the horizon for much of the winter.

This is called the **polar night**.

People in Norway, Finland, Sweden, and Greenland can all encounter polar nights.

This is a winter afternoon in Tromso, in Norway.

In winter, the polar night in Tromso lasts for 60 days. It is dark in the daytime and it is dark at night.

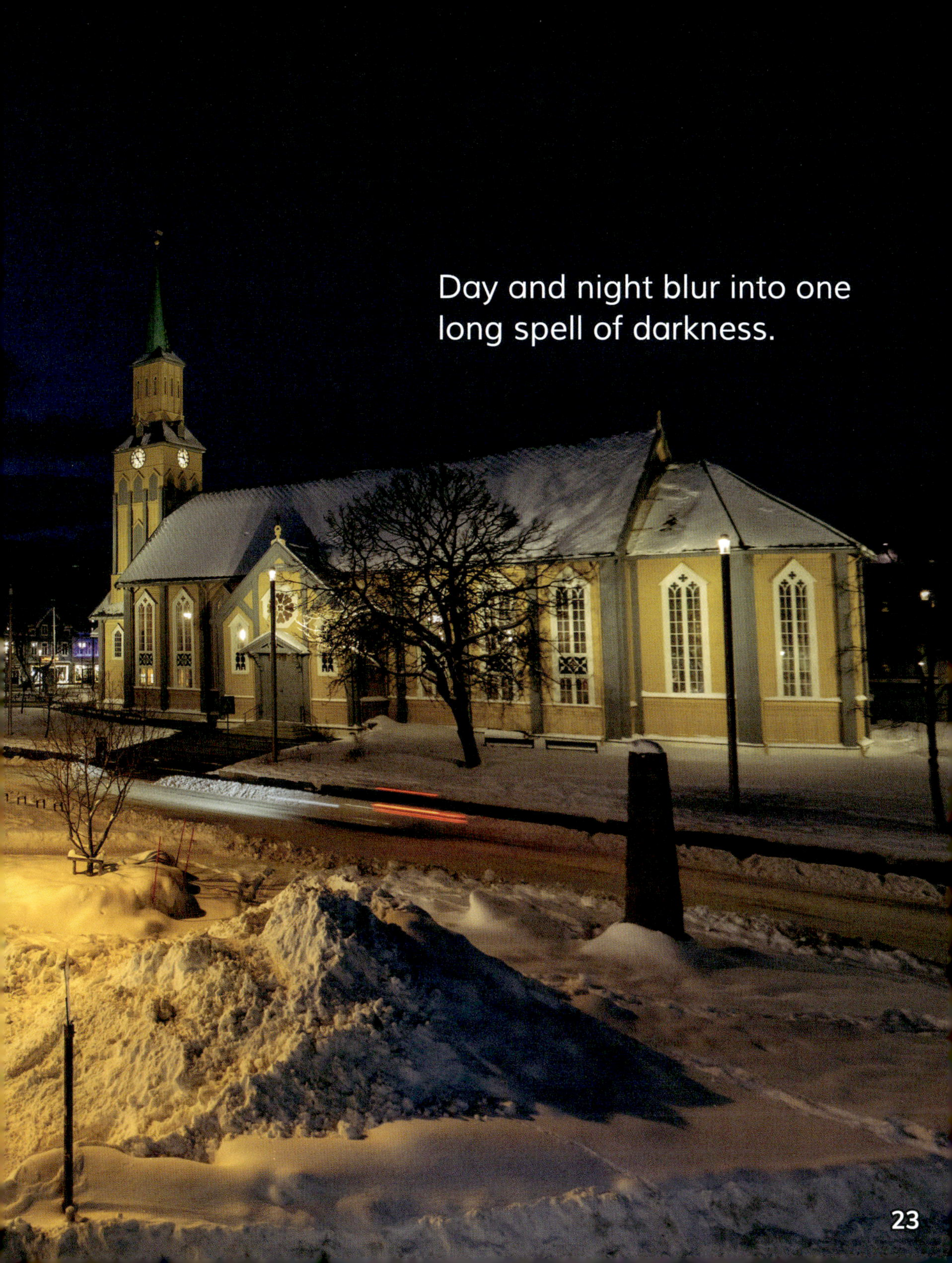

Day and night blur into one long spell of darkness.

As well as living through the long polar nights, you might get to see the Northern Lights as well.

It can be quite spectacular!

If you are in the Arctic or the Antarctic in the summertime, the sun may never go below the horizon.

Now the days and the nights are light all the time. It's like a permanent day.

People say that this is the **polar day**. They say it is the land of the midnight sun.

So, in the wintertime, it is dark all day – then, in the summertime, it is light all day.

These flowers are catching the midnight sun in Svalbard, in Norway.

In Svalbard, there is no sunset for 126 days in a year! It can be hard to get to sleep at night.

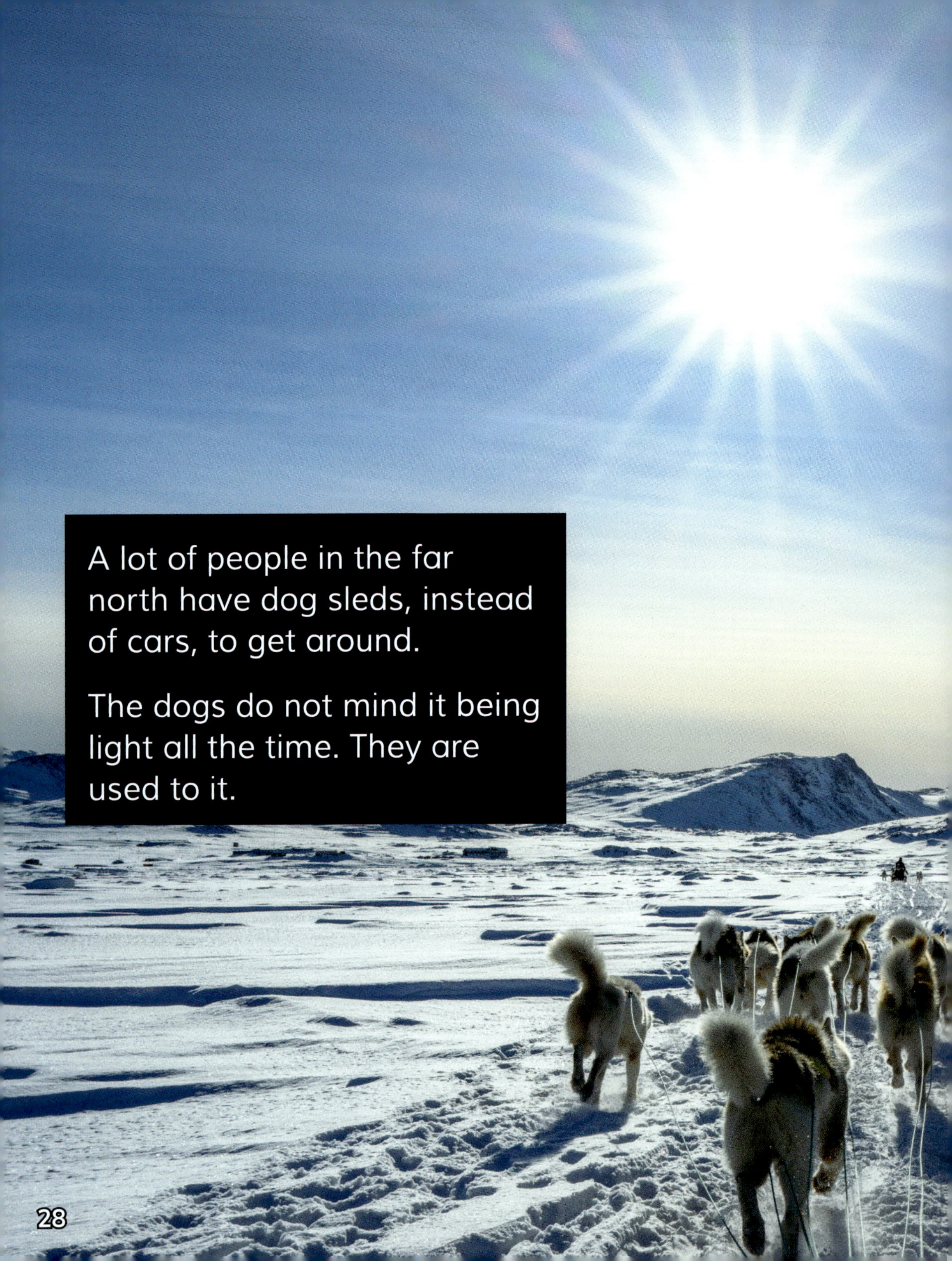

A lot of people in the far north have dog sleds, instead of cars, to get around.

The dogs do not mind it being light all the time. They are used to it.

The wildlife too must cope with the permanent light and dark of the polar days and nights.

This is Murmansk, a big port in the Arctic.

In Murmansk, the polar night lasts 40 days. Then it sees the midnight sun for 63 days.

The smoke from the chimneys is not a help in the polar nights!

Do you find it hard to get up on cold, dark winter mornings?

Then I think the polar nights are not for you.